TO THE TEACHER

In my many years of teaching piano to the young I have found that the theory of music, so necessary for good performance and musicianship, is best learned and **retained** through written work.

The lessons herewith have been used with excellent results and at the request of countless teachers met during my many workshops I am now making them available herewith in printed form.

They are designed to supply written work that will make plainer than plain the facts in learning about music. Actually, theory is the language of music and to perform well one must speak and understand this "language" without hestitation.

The written work will not only train the student to observe carefully and to be accurate in what he does but will also serve as a help to the teacher in checking the student's comprehension of what he is learning.

The work progresses gradually and is planned to be suitable for use with any method or series of teaching materials either in class or private instruction.

It is suggested that these lessons be given the student one at a time.

EDNA MAE BURNAM

ISBN 978-7-4234-0600-6

Exclusively Distributed By

Visit Hal Leonard Online at
www.halleonard.com

World headquarters, contact:
Hal Leonard
7777 West Bluemound Road
Milwaukee, WI 53213
Email: info@halleonard.com

In Europe, contact:
Hal Leonard Europe Limited
1 Red Place
London, W1K 6PL
Email: info@halleonardeurope.com

In Australia, contact:
Hal Leonard Australia Pty. Ltd.
4 Lentara Court
Cheltenham, Victoria, 3192 Australia
Email: info@halleonard.com.au

RUDIMENTS

treble clef
bass clef
bar line
double bar
measure

NOTES

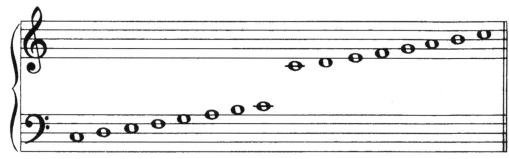

NOTE AND REST VALUES

quarter
half
dotted half
whole
eighth

TIME SIGNATURES

$\frac{2}{4}$ $\frac{3}{4}$ $\frac{4}{4}$

NOTE MOVEMENT AND NOTE LOCATION

notes moving up.
notes moving down.
line notes.
space notes.
the MUSICAL ALPHABET forwards, and backwards.

SIGNS

hold
accent
staccato
repeat
sharp
flat
natural

KEY SIGNATURES

C Major
F Major
G Major

WORD	ABBREVIATION	MEANING
forte	f	loud
mezzo forte	mf	medium loud
fortissimo	ff	very loud
piano	p	soft
mezzo piano	mp	medium soft
pianissimo	pp	very soft
ritard	$rit.$	gradually slower

LESSON ONE

Pupil's Name _____ **Date** _____ **Grade (or Star)** _____

1. READING

As you read each note, print its letter name in the box above or below it.

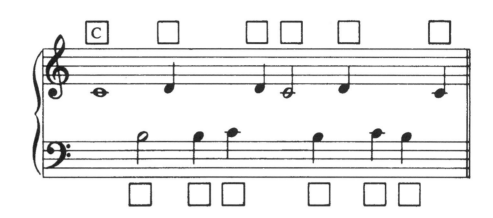

2. WRITING

Write the note for each letter printed in the boxes.

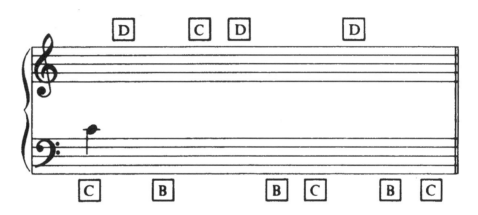

3. COUNTING

Count the number of beats and write the total in each box.

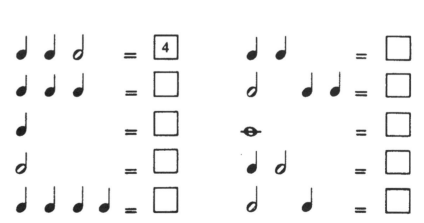

4. SPELLING

Say aloud the letter name of each note.

5. DRAWING

Below is an example of how the treble clef sign is drawn.

Draw a line downward.	Draw a curve to the X.	Draw a curve to this X.	Make a loop to the X as above.	And now a curly-cue with a dot on the end

After practicing on scratch paper draw a row of treble clefs here.

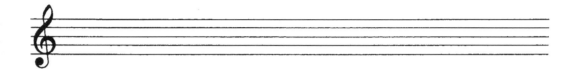

Below is an example of how the bass clef sign is drawn.

Make a dot on the line above.	Draw a curve to the X.	Draw another curve to the X above.	Make a dot on each side of the line the X crosses.

After practicing on scratch paper draw a row of bass clefs here.

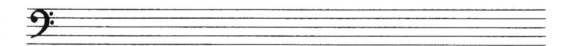

6. GAME

CRISS-CROSS RUNS.

Draw a line from the words to their matching music symbols. The treble clef is done for you as a "helper".

Some of the lines will criss-cross.

Treble clef.

Bass clef.

Bar line.

Time signature.

Double bar.

Whole note.

Half note.

Quarter note

Measure.

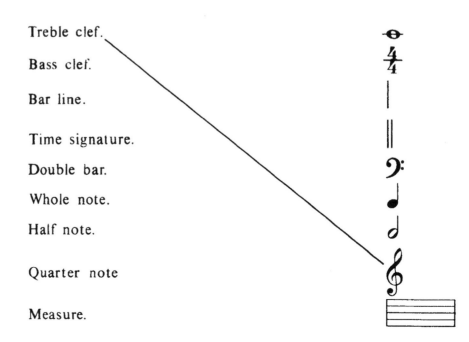

LESSON TWO

Pupil's Name _____ Date _____ Grade (or Star) _____

1. READING

As you read each note, print its letter name in the box above or below it.

2. WRITING

Write the note for each letter printed in the boxes.

3. COUNTING

Count the number of beats and write the total in each box.

4. SPELLING

The letter names of these notes spell words. Write them in the boxes under the notes.

5. DRAWING

Draw an arrow showing notes moving upward and also for notes moving downward.

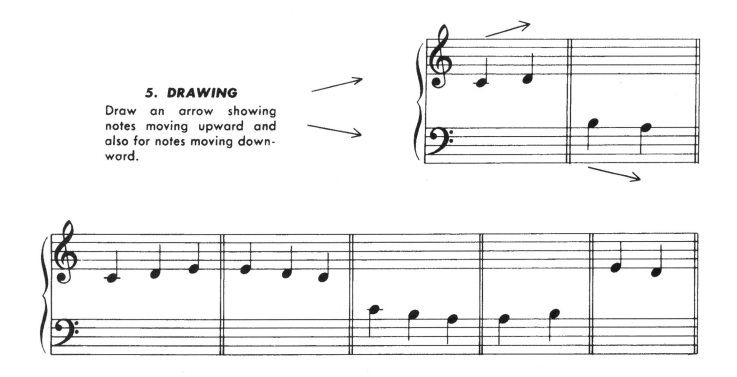

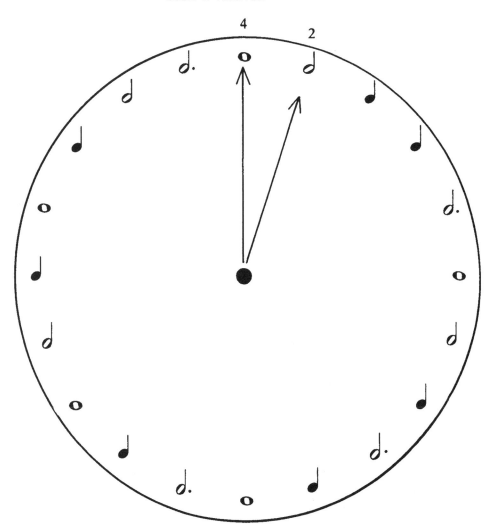

6. GAME
SHOOTING ARROWS

Draw an arrow to each note and write the number of beats it receives.

LESSON THREE

Pupil's Name _____ Date _____ Grade (or Star) _____

1. READING
As you read each note, print its letter name in the box above or below it.

C ☐ ☐ ☐   ☐   ☐ ☐   ☐

☐ ☐ ☐ ☐   ☐ ☐   ☐

2. WRITING
Write the note for each letter printed in the boxes.

F D E   F   E D

G   A B C   G   C

3. COUNTING
Count the number of beats and write the total in each box.

HELPER

Quarter Rest 𝄾 . . . . 1 beat

Half Rest ▬ . . . . . . 2 beats

Whole Measure Rest ⧙3/4 ▬⧘ . . . . . 3 beats

⧙4/4 ▬⧘ . . . . . . 4 beats

▬ ♩ ♩ = 4

♩ 𝄾 ♩ ♩ = ☐

♩ 𝄾 𝄾 = ☐

4/4 ▬ = ☐

3/4 ▬ = ☐

▬ 𝅗𝅥 = ☐

4. SPELLING
The letter names of these notes spell words.
Write them in the boxes under the notes.

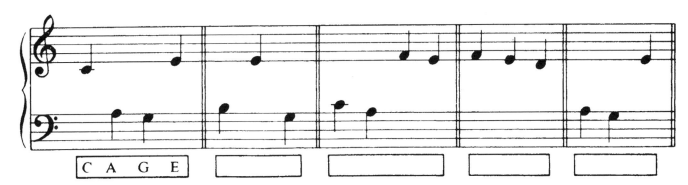

C A G E   ☐   ☐   ☐   ☐

5. DRAWING
Below is an example of how a Quarter Rest is drawn.

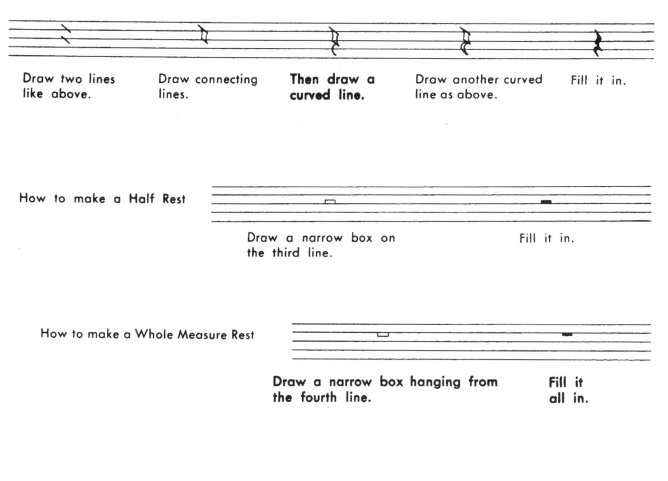

Draw two lines like above.   Draw connecting lines.   **Then draw a curved line.**   Draw another curved line as above.   Fill it in.

How to make a Half Rest

Draw a narrow box on the third line.   Fill it in.

How to make a Whole Measure Rest

Draw a narrow box hanging from the fourth line.   **Fill it all in.**

Draw 4 more Quarter Rests.   Draw 4 more Half Rests.   Draw 4 more Whole Measure Res

6. GAME
FINDING PARTNERS

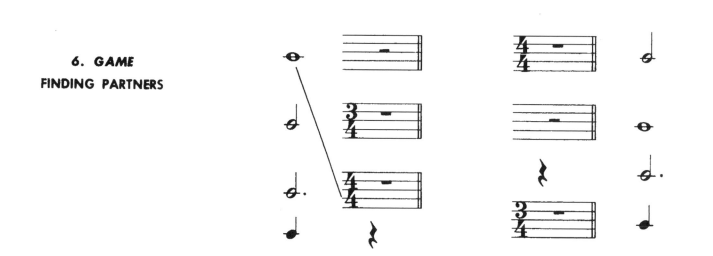

Draw a line from each note to its matching rest.   Draw a line from each rest to its matching note.

LESSON FOUR

Pupil's Name _____ Date _____ Grade (or Star) _____

1. READING

As you read each note, print its letter name in the box above or below it.

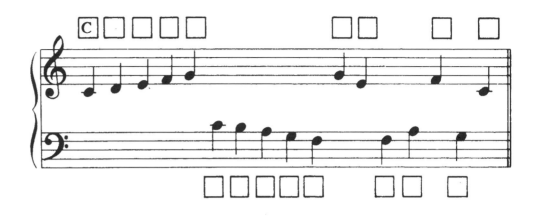

2. WRITING

Write the note for each letter printed in the boxes.

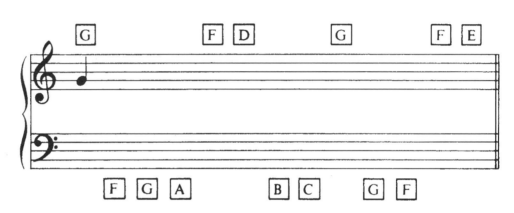

3. COUNTING

In each box write the note or rest that will give the total counts shown by the numbers.

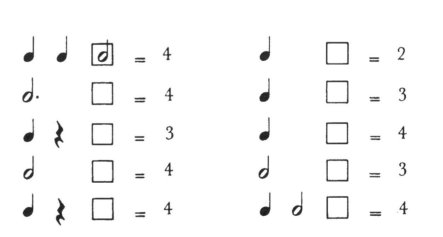

4. SPELLING

The letter names of these notes spell names. Write them in the boxes below.

5. DRAWING

Draw a circle around every Quarter Rest.

Draw a triangle around every Half Rest.

Draw a square around every Whole Measure Rest

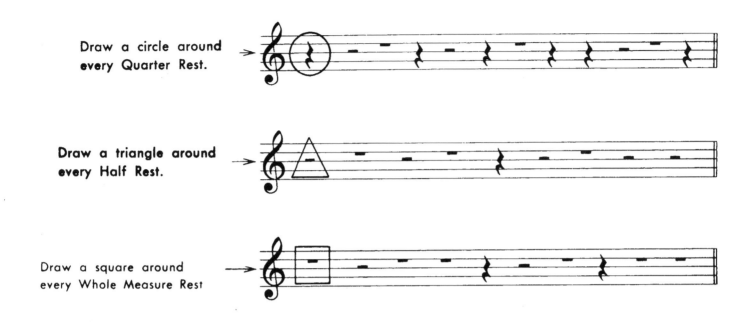

6. GAME

FOLLOW THE LEADER.

Copy these notes here ____

Copy these notes here ____

Copy these notes here ____

Copy these notes here ____

BOOK ONE

LESSON FIVE

Pupil's Name _____ Date _____ Grade (or Star) _____

1. READING

As you read each note, print its letter name in the box above or below it.

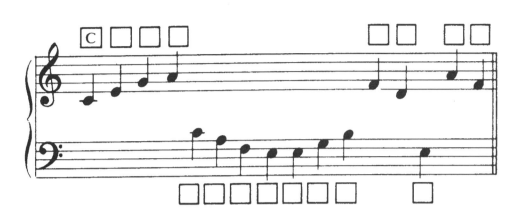

2. WRITING

Write the note for each letter printed in the boxes.

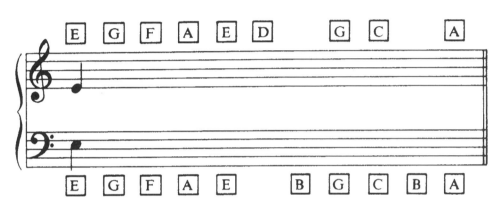

3. COUNTING

Draw bar lines in each of these three different time signatures and put the number of counts under each measure.

4. SPELLING

The letter names of these notes spell words. Write them in the boxes below.

HELPERS

5. DRAWING

In music, notes are written on either lines or spaces.

These are LINE NOTES. The lines run through the middle of the notes.

These are SPACE NOTES. The notes are placed between the lines.

LEGER LINE NOTES.

A LEGER LINE is a short line used for a note that is not on the staff. Middle C is on a leger line so is classified as a line note.

Draw a square around every space note.

Draw a circle around every line note.

6. GAME

WATCH THOSE LINES

Team A and Team B have line and space notes.

Count the line notes each Team has and write the total in the box at the end.

Write the letter of the winning Team in the circle.

BOOK ONE
LESSON SIX

Pupil's Name _____ Date _____ Grade (or Star) _____

HELPER — Read this ALOUD!
For notes on the THIRD LINE of the treble or bass staff
the stems may go either UP or DOWN.

1. READING

As you read each note, print its letter name in the box above or below it.

2. WRITING

Write the note for each letter printed in the boxes.

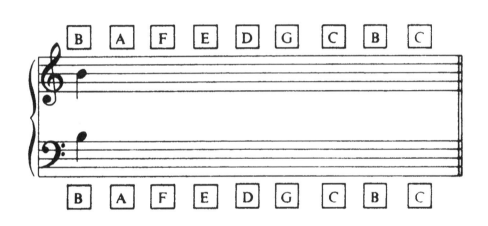

3. COUNTING

Count the number of beats and write the total in each box.

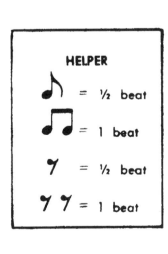

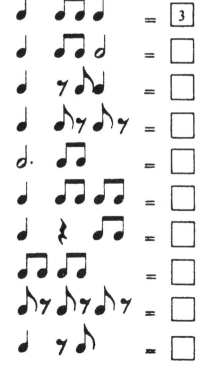

4. SPELLING

Say aloud the letter names of the
MUSIC ALPHABET as you play this music.

LINE
A

A B C D E F G A A A A A

Say aloud the letter names of the
MUSIC ALPHABET BACKWARDS as
you play this music.

LINE
B

G F E D C B A G F E D C B A A A A

5. DRAWING

In LINE A draw an arrow over the notes of the musical alphabet that go upwards.

In LINE B draw an arrow under the notes of the musical alphabet that go downwards.

6. GAME

NAME THE MISSING NOTE!

There are many notes on the treble and bass staffs below.

Print the letter name of each note in the box above or below each note.

There is one note missing from the complete MUSIC ALPHABET. Which one is it?

Write the name of the missing note in the circle.

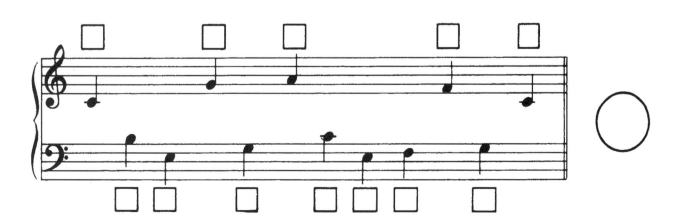

LESSON SEVEN

Pupil's Name _____ Date _____ Grade (or Star) _____

1. READING

As you read each note, print its letter name in the box above or below it.

> **HELPER — Read this aloud!**
>
> On the treble staff, notes ABOVE the THIRD LINE have stems going DOWN on the left side of the note.
>
> On the bass staff, notes BELOW the THIRD LINE have stems going UP on the right side of the note.

2. WRITING

Write the abbreviation for the following.

forte _____

piano _____

ritard _____

mezzo forte _____

pianissimo _____

mezzo piano _____

fortissimo _____

HELPER		
WORD	ABBREVIATION	MEANING
ritard	*rit.*	gradually slower
forte	*f*	loud
mezzo forte	*mf*	medium loud
fortissimo	*ff*	very loud
piano	*p*	soft
mezzo piano	*mp*	medium soft
pianissimo	*pp*	very soft

3. COUNTING

Draw bar lines in each of these three different time signatures and put the number of counts under each measure.

4. SPELLING

Spell correctly as you print the abbreviations for the following:

medium soft _____

gradually slower _____

medium loud _____

loud _____

very loud _____

soft _____

very soft _____

5. DRAWING

Here is an example of how an EIGHTH
REST is made. An EIGHTH REST looks
like the number 7.

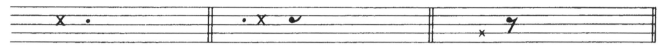

Make a dot on the
space marked by the X.

Draw a curved line
to this X.

Draw a slightly slanted
line to this X.

Draw EIGHTH NOTES as examples below.

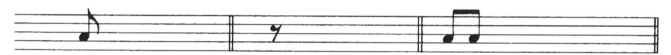

Draw 4 more eighth
notes like the one above.

Draw 4 more eighth rests
like the one above.

Draw 4 more groups of 2 eighth
notes like those above.

6. GAME

MYSTERY TUNE.

This is the beginning of a
well-known tune. Sing it to
yourself (not playing the
notes). Write the name of
the tune in the box above
the music.

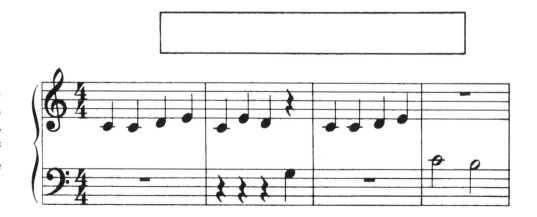

LESSON EIGHT

Pupil's Name _____ Date _____ Grade (or Star) _____

1. READING

This is a SHARP sign ♯

The slanting box in the middle is on the same line or space as the note it is sharping.

The closed part of this SHARP sign is filled in to make the above point clear.

A sharp

This is a NATURAL sign ♮

The slanting box in the middle is on the same line or space as the note it is making natural.

The closed part of this NATURAL sign is filled in to make the above point clear.

F natural

This is a FLAT sign ♭

The open space that looks like half of a heart is on the same line or space as the note it is flatting.

The closed part of this FLAT sign is filled in to make the above point clear.

E Flat

Check the right answers as you read the following:

This is a ♭ { SHARP
              FLAT
              NATURAL

This is a ♮ { SHARP
              FLAT
              NATURAL

This is a ♯ { SHARP
              FLAT
              NATURAL

2. WRITING

Here is a line of SHARP, FLAT and NATURAL signs.

In the box below each sign write:

S for SHARP

F for FLAT

N for NATURAL

♯ ♭ ♮ ♭ ♮ ♯ ♭ ♯ ♮ ♭

| S | | | | | | | | | |

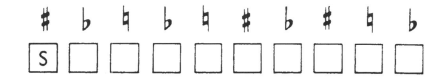

3. COUNTING

Put in the TIME SIGNATURES and number the counting under each measure.

4. SPELLING

Print the correctly spelled words in the boxes to complete each sentence.

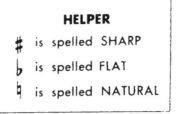

HELPER

♯ is spelled SHARP

♭ is spelled FLAT

♮ is spelled NATURAL

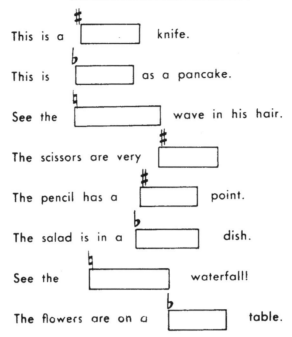

This is a [♯] knife.

This is [♭] as a pancake.

See the [♮] wave in his hair.

The scissors are very [♯].

The pencil has a [♯] point.

The salad is in a [♭] dish.

See the [♮] waterfall!

The flowers are on a [♭] table.

5. DRAWING

With a pencil, fill in all the closed parts of the SHARPS, FLATS and NATURALS. Then print the letter name of each sign in the box above or below it.

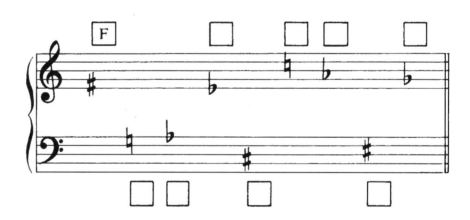

6. GAME

TIC-TAC-TOE.

Find 3 of the same signs in a row. They may be VERTICAL, HORIZONTAL or DIAGONAL.

Make a line through them when you find them, then print the name of the winner in the box below it.

♯	♭	♭
♮	♯	♮
♭	♮	♯

SHARP

♯	♮	♭
♯	♭	♯
♭	♭	♮

♭	♯	♭
♭	♮	♭
♯	♯	♭

♯	♯	♭
♮	♮	♭
♯	♯	♯

♯	♭	♯
♮	♮	♮
♭	♯	♭

LESSON NINE

Pupil's Name _____ Date _____ Grade (or Star) _____

1. READING

READ THIS ALOUD!

This is the key signature of C MAJOR.

There are no sharps nor flats in the key of C MAJOR.

C MAJOR

READ THIS ALOUD!

This is the key signature of F MAJOR.

There is one flat (B flat) in the key of F MAJOR.

F MAJOR

READ THIS ALOUD!

This is the key signature of G MAJOR.

There is one sharp (F sharp) in the key of G MAJOR.

G MAJOR

2. WRITING

Write the name of the key signature in the box under each measure.

3. COUNTING

Fill in each box with one note or rest to make the correct number of beats in each measure.

4. DRAWING

To draw a SHARP sign:

Draw a line downwards like this |

Then begin a little higher
and draw another line like this ||

Draw two lines crossing the
first lines like this ♯

To draw a NATURAL sign:

Draw a line downwards like this |

Then draw **two short lines like this** ⊢

Then draw another line like this ♮

To draw a FLAT sign:

Draw a line downwards |

Then start in the middle
of the line and curve
around to the bottom
of the line. ♭

Draw 4 more sharp signs.

♯

Draw 4 more flat signs.

♭

Draw 4 more natural signs.

♮

5. SPELLING

These notes spell words. Print the letter names of them in the boxes under them.

In the circles, print the letter S if all the letter names of the notes are SPACE notes and the letter L if all the letter names of the notes are LINE notes.

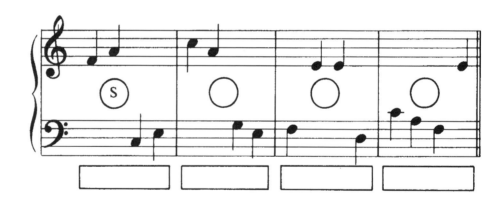

6. GAME

MYSTERY TUNE.

This is the beginning of a well-known tune. Sing it to yourself (not playing the notes.) Write the name of the tune in the long box above the music.

BOOK ONE
LESSON TEN

Pupil's Name _____ Date _____ Grade (or Star) _____

1. READING

Check the right answers
as you read the following:

HELPER — Read this aloud!

This is a HOLD sign

This is an ACCENT sign

This is a REPEAT sign

This is a STACCATO sign

This is a REPEAT sign

This is a HOLD sign

This is an ACCENT sign

This is a STACCATO sign

2. WRITING

Write the note for the letter
printed in each box.

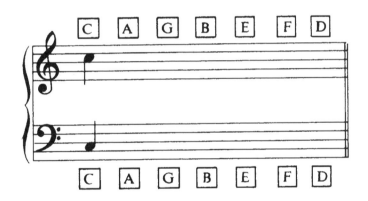

| C | A | G | B | E | F | D |

3. COUNTING

Fill in each box with one note
or rest to make the correct
number of beats in each
measure.

4. SPELLING

The musical symbol above each box represents a musical term. Write it in each box to complete the sentence.

This is a [ ] plate.

I like to [ ] happy.

I like the [ ] letter opener!

She is a [ ] Blonde.

5. DRAWING

Draw the musical signs for the following

HOLD _____

REPEAT _____

ACCENT _____

STACCATO _____

6. GAME

HOP SCOTCH.

Here are two HOP SCOTCH patterns.

Fill in HOP SCOTCH pattern number II with notes to match the rests in HOP SCOTCH pattern number I.

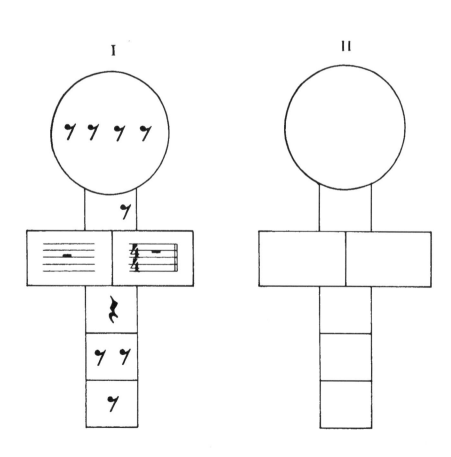

LESSON ELEVEN

Pupil's Name _____ Date _____ Grade (or Star) _____

THE LION

1. READING

The notes in each measure spell a word in these two poems. Read them aloud!

The lion in 🎼 🎼 at the Zoo,

Is 🎼 at half past two!

He really eats 🎼 great big 🎼

Of 🎼 and other things too!

THE PARTY

I went to 🎼 party, and who did I see?

🎼 and 🎼 and 🎼 and 🎼

We played 🎼 game with 🎼 prize for me,

Had cake, ice cream, and fun, OH 🎼 !

2. WRITING

Write the notes for each letter printed in the boxes.

| F | A | E | B | D | G | F | C |

| F | E | A | D | B | F | G | C |

3. SPELLING

These FLAT, SHARP and NATURAL signs spell words.

Print them in the boxes below each measure.

24

4. COUNTING

Count the SHARP signs in this line and write the total in the box at the end of the line.

♯ ♭ ♮ ♯ ♮ ♭ ♯ ♮ ♭ ♯ ♮ ♭ ☐

Count the FLAT signs in this line and write the total in the box at the end of the line.

♭ ♯ ♮ ♭ ♭ ♭ ♮ ♯ ♮ ♭ ♯ ♭ ☐

Count the NATURAL signs in this line and write the total in the box at the end of the line.

♮ ♯ ♭ ♭ ♮ ♯ ♮ ♭ ♭ ♯ ♮ ♮ ♭ ☐

5. DRAWING

Draw an arrow from each word to its matching partner.

Hold	⟶	⌢
Accent		∶‖
Repeat		*p*
Staccato		>
Very soft		*f*
Very loud		*pp*
Soft		.
Medium soft		*ff*
Medium loud		*mf*
Gradually slower		*mp*
Loud		*rit.*

6. GAME

MYSTERY TUNE.

This is the beginning of a well-known tune. Sing it to yourself. DON'T PLAY THE NOTES!

Write the name of the tune in the box above the music.

BOOK ONE
LESSON TWELVE

Pupil's Name _____ Date _____ Grade (or Star) _____

1. READING

As you read each note, print its letter name in the box above or below it.

2. WRITING

If a note is on a SPACE write an S in the box above or below it.

If a note is on a LINE write an L in the box above or below it.

3. COUNTING

Write in the number of notes or rests needed to have:

3 beats in No. 1

2 beats in No. 2

4 beats in No. 3

Each line must be DIFFERENT, as in the HELPER.

HELPER

Study this before doing the exercises.

1. ♩ ♩ ♩ ♩   = 4

2. ♩ ♩   = 4

3. ♩ 𝄽 ♩   = 4

4. ♩ ▬   = 4

No. 1

1.	=	3
2.	=	3
3.	=	3
4.	=	3

No. 2

1.	=	2
2.	=	2
3.	=	2
4.	=	2

No. 3

1.	=	4
2.	=	4
3.	=	4
4.	=	4

4. SPELLING

Write the abbreviations for these musical terms:

Gradually slower _____

Very loud _____

Very soft _____

Medium loud _____

Medium soft _____

Soft _____

Loud _____

5. DRAWING

Draw the following:

Eighth note	Accent
Eighth rest	Bass clef
Quarter note	Hold
Quarter rest	Repeat
Whole note	Sharp
Whole measure rest	Flat
Treble clef	Natural

6. GAME

CATCH ME IF YOU CAN!

Put a check mark like this X after the correct answer for each of the following:

>
- Hold
- Accent X
- Staccato

𝄾
- Quarter rest
- Half rest
- Eighth rest

♪
- Quarter note
- Half note
- Eighth note

:‖
- Bar line
- Bass clef
- Repeat

𝄞
- Treble clef
- Bass clef
- Bar line

(treble clef, one flat)
- F Major
- C Major
- G Major

(treble clef, no accidentals)
- F Major
- C Major
- G Major

(treble clef, one sharp)
- F Major
- C Major
- G Major

ff
- Very soft
- Very loud

(line note)
- Line note
- Space note

(notes)
- Notes moving UP
- Notes moving DOWN

♮
- Sharp
- Flat
- Natural

NOTES

NOTES